all emotions are OK

Written by
Dr Sarah Temple

Illustrated by
Sarah-Leigh Wills

There are 3 coloured sections in this book

Children   Tools   Science

Foreword

The aim of this book is to help you as parents and caregivers to talk about emotions and feelings, so that you can support the normal development of your children and the children in your communities. We call this emotion coaching.

In an article in The Daily Express on 29th June 2020, Kate Middleton and Prince William spoke of how they liked to resolve their children's issues through an open discussion using emotional coaching. The couple said "The children are encouraged to talk about their feelings".

At stressful times, instead of punishing or dismissing a child, the emotion coaching approach involves emotionally connecting with the child, discussing and exploring feelings, labelling emotions and reflecting on them before problem solving. **Emotion coaching was first described by John Gottman - Professor Emeritus in Psychology at Washington University.** Emotional connection together with problem solving and limit setting supports the child to regulate their emotions and find a way forward from the situation they are struggling with. Emotion coaching calls for parents and caregivers to develop insight into their own emotions (emotion literacy).

Key to developing our emotion literacy as adults is understanding a metaphor of emotion regulation put together by Daniel J. Siegel - Professor of Psychiatry at the UCLA School of Medicine in Los Angeles. This explains how when something causes us to 'flip our lid', we may cry, shout, lash out, freeze, run away or withdraw into ourselves. Our rational, logical thinking is being overwhelmed by our emotions, making it hard to think clearly. This is when we can say and do things we wouldn't normally do or that aren't OK. We can learn to notice our emotions earlier and make changes so that we 'flip our lids' less often. We can then support children and young people to manage their emotions and behaviours.

You will find information for parents, carers and adult caregivers where you see this bubble as well as practical ideas to support developing emotion intelligence and emotion literacy.

"This is a fantastic book about how to be more accepting of your child's emotions, including the negative ones, and allows parents the freedom to realise that their job is not to keep their child happy at all times. It is full of practical advice about how to talk to your child about their emotions.
I can't recommend it highly enough".

Dr John Lambie, Associate Professor of Psychology,
Author of My First Emotions.

The next few pages
have been created
for you to read
together as a family

Emotions are feelings that we all have. Things like:

anger   fear

sadness   surprise

joy   disgust

contempt

All emotions and feelings are OK but not all behaviours are OK. This book will help you manage your feelings and emotions and work out ways to understand yourself.

Did you know that everyone has emotions and feelings and that they usually begin with changes in your body? You can get better at noticing them.

There is a very clever doctor in America called Daniel Siegel who has worked out a way to make it easy to talk about big feelings and emotions.

The Wholebrain Child Workbook - practical exercises and activities to help you manage your emotions.
Daniel J. Siegel MD
Tina Payne Bryson PhD

Douglas flips his lid!

When Douglas is feeling calm and happy his lid is down

But sometimes when his feelings get really big he can flip his lid

We're going to help you learn to notice when your lid is flapping and bring it down before it flips

Think about when you're feeling calm and well – this might be doing a favourite thing like painting or colouring or building with Lego. It could be dribbling a football or learning to juggle.

Mindful activities can be fun! Think of things you can do as a parent that involve using your body and focusing your attention at the same time. The more you do, the more the children around you will do.

Hold your hand up with your fist closed – this represents feeling calm and well. Now raise your fingers up so that your thumb is uncovered – this represents your lid flapping.
Move your fingers up further until they are pointing upwards– this is your lid flipping.
Mindful activities help us bring our lids down.

There are lots of different things you can do to feel calm and happy. The important thing is to work out what works for you and do plenty of it. Being outside in nature, eating healthily, sleeping well and exercising are all things that help us feel good about ourselves.

An example of self-care is having healthy sleeping habits such as quitting social media an hour before bed.

Now think about a moment when you felt really out of control and you flipped your lid. You might have felt taken over with angry feelings, sad feelings or worry feelings.

When you get these really strong feelings it can be hard to be kind to yourself and to others around you. Sometimes you might say things you wouldn't normally say or do things you wouldn't normally do. The best thing to do is try hard to notice when the feelings start and calm yourself down before you flip your lid.

Can you say out loud how you feel in your body before you get taken over by big feelings and flip your lid?

You might remember things like feeling tight and tense all over, a hurting tummy or feeling tingly.

Sometimes it can be hard talking about feelings.

Last time Mum nearly flipped her lid with Douglas was when he was getting ready for school.

Just as she was about to start shouting 'HURRY UP'
in a really cross voice she remembered to
PAUSE and slow down her breathing.

Mum noticed she felt tense all
over- especially in her tummy.

Mum was feeling all mixed up and very confused. She felt sad and angry all at the same time. She felt big feelings of worry that they would be late for school and she felt tired too.

Mum slowed down her breathing and noticed
the air going in and out of her body.

She ran her finger along the fingers on her
other hand breathing in and out slowly.

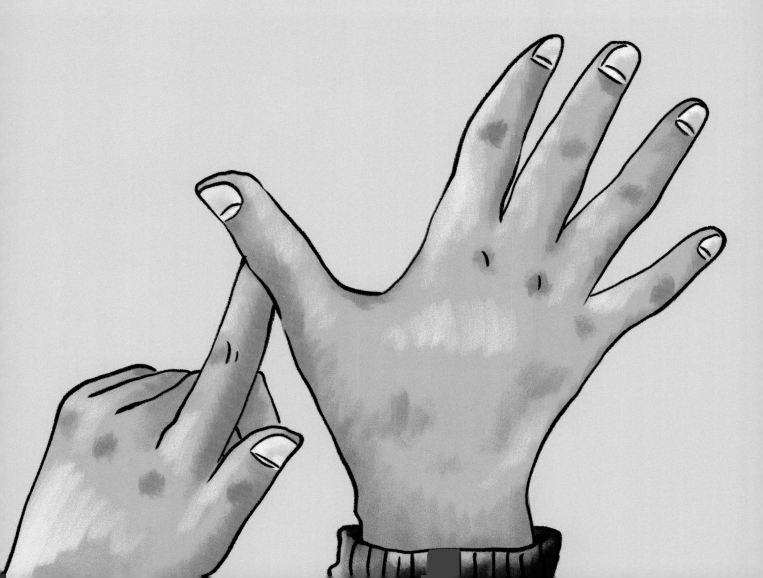

Mum said out loud that she was feeling tense in her tummy and that she felt all mixed up with worry feelings and sad feelings too.

Douglas saw Mum was calming down. He noticed his tummy was tense too.

He took a deep breath and slowly filled up. He put his hand on his tummy and felt it get bigger.

He let out a long breath and noticed he was feeling better.

Mum had her lid down and said:
'I think you might be worrying about something – am I right? Shall we talk a bit more about your feelings over breakfast?'

Douglas talked about his jumbled up feelings, his fed up feelings and his worry feelings. Sometimes, he said, his worry feelings just don't seem to go away.

Then he talked about his friend Ben who he loves to see.

How do you think Douglas is feeling now?

Try and notice your feelings and emotions before they get too big and do something that makes you feel calm and well. Sometimes having a favourite pebble in your pocket that you can touch or slowing down and concentrating on your breathing or on the sensation of your feet on the floor can really help.

There are lots of ideas for ways the grown ups around you can help on the next few pages

Tools and resources

1. Talking about emotions

2. Noticing emotions

3. Being aware of warning signs

4. Knowing what makes you feel calm and content

5. Creating a glitter jar

6. Going on a mindful walk

Emotion Words

We know from research by Paul Ekman that there are seven core emotions that humans everywhere in the world experience and these are: anger, sadness, surprise, joy, disgust, fear and contempt. Try and think of as many different ways as you can of talking about these core emotions.

We have lots of resources to help you talk about emotions www.mindfulemotioncoaching.co.uk

Remember physical sensations in the body are important too!

Noticing

Try linking your feelings signals with one of the seven core emotions common to all of us

anger, sadness, surprise, joy, disgust, fear, contempt

- explosive
- grateful
- hurt
- ignored
- relaxed
- excited
- helpless
- confused
- unsafe
- resentful
- left out
- comfortable
- anxious
- alone
- worried
- abandoned

Noticing

Try linking your body signals with one of the seven core emotions common to all of us

anger, sadness, surprise, joy, disgust, fear, contempt

- tired for no reason
- tense muscles
- butterflies in your tummy
- sick in the stomach
- felt like crying
- clenched fists
- breathing fast
- sweaty
- heart thumping
- jittery or jumpy
- lump in throat

Glitter Jar

Find a clean plastic bottle with a lid and half fill it with water

Add plenty of liquid glue and some food colouring

Add glitter – choose whatever colour you prefer
or lots of different colours

Put on the bottle top

When you start to feel your warning signs
that big emotions are on their way, shake
the bottle and breathe slowly while the
glitter settles to the bottom.

Mindful Walk

This is my favourite mindful exercise and it's easy to do wherever you are:

- Take one long, slow breath, breathing in through the nose and out through the mouth

- Stand with your feet hip-width apart

- Gently lean your body forward

- Notice your weight shift to the balls of your feet

- Notice your toes gripping the ground

- Breathe slowly and notice the air move in and out of your airways

- Bring your attention back to the balls of your feet and your toes

- Count 10 seconds and gently shift your weight back so you are standing upright or move forwards into a very slow walk

- Take a long, slow breath, in through the nose and out through the mouth

Mindful exercises like this bring your lid down and stimulate your vagus nerve. This nerve runs from the bottom of your brain all through your body and slows things like your heart rate and breathing rate.

For parents, carers and caregivers

'We know from the science that the more we can help our children to recognise and express their emotions the easier they will find it to make friends and feel comfortable with themselves'. Dr Sarah Temple MRCGP, Director EHCAP Ltd

There is a critical period from conception through to about 3 years not only for laying down of pathways in the brain but also for the immune system, metabolic system and genetic expression. **So this isn't just about early learning in school - it's about the foundations of lifelong physical and mental health**. It's about decreasing the likelihood that your child will develop heart disease or hypertension, or diabetes, or a wide range of the most common chronic illnesses in society.

After birth and in the first two years, neurones connect as they take up sensory information - more than one million new connections are formed every second in an infant's brain. Your child's brain will continue to develop into their mid 20s - in other words **it's never too late to support your child's healthy brain development**. Having at least one parent or carer able to emotion coach is an important contributor to healthy brain development. This is relevant for all children but especially for highly sensitive children with neurodiversities such as high functioning autism. This is because these children may be more susceptible to the effects of stress.

Healthy relationships protect the developing child from adversity and promote healthy brain circuits. Research from Center on the Developing Child, Harvard University helps us understand the biological response to stress through a description of **Positive, Tolerable and Toxic stress responses**. The physiological response to toxic stress causes stress hormone levels to rise, activates the inflammatory phase of the immune system, affects metabolic regulation, disrupts brain architecture (fear circuits, executive function, emotion regulation) and affects molecular turning on and off of genes. We know that inflammation underpins many of the most common diseases throughout life and a prolonged inflammatory response early in life can accelerate heart disease, depression, arthritis and other chronic illnesses. The body's toxic stress response is buffered by emotion coaching relationships with other people.

A **Positive Stress response** is a normal and essential part of life. It is characterised by brief increases in heart rate and mild elevations in hormone levels. Examples include things like getting to an appointment on time, getting children ready for school or preparing for a deadline. Experiencing positive stress responses in childhood enables normal development.

A **Tolerable Stress response** occurs when the body's stress response systems are activated at a higher level - for instance by more severe, longer lasting difficulties, such as the loss of a loved one, a natural disaster, or a frightening injury. **With a tolerable stress response the effects of the activation of the body's stress response are buffered by relationships. Emotion coaching interactions with an adult caregiver help children adapt so that the developing brain and other organs are able to recover from what might otherwise be damaging effects.**

A **Toxic Stress response** occurs when the body's stress response systems are activated at a higher level with strong, frequent and/or prolonged adversity including neglect and abuse as well as exposure to violence. **Crucially, without buffering emotion coaching style relationships the stress response systems are activated at a level that can cause long term physiological changes.** Stress hormone levels rise, the inflammatory phase of the immune system is activated, metabolic regulation is affected, brain architecture (fear circuits, executive function, emotion regulation) is disrupted and molecular turning on and off of genes is affected. In other words, a Toxic Stress response changes how cells work together.

Dr Sarah Temple began working on this trauma informed, healing centered approach to wellness in 2010. The approach is based on John Gottman's Emotion Coaching, Daniel J. Siegel's metaphors and research from Center on the Developing Child, Harvard University. Mindful Emotion Coaching is particularly relevant at the moment as a compassionate response to stress families have experienced during the coronavirus pandemic (2020-21).

Professor John Gottman's observational research (1997) shows that where parents use an Emotion Coaching Style for at least 30% of the time their children achieve more academically at school, are more popular with their peers, have fewer infectious illnesses, have fewer behavioural problems, are more emotionally stable and are more able to cope with life's ups and downs.

Raising an Emotionally Intelligent Child – The Heart of Parenting by John Gottman PhD with Joan Declaire.

Emotion Coaching

Professor John Gottman describes four relationship styles:

Emotion Dismissive Style - 'don't worry, you'll be fine'

Emotion Disapproving Style - 'if you hadn't gone out yesterday and you'd done some work you...'

Laissez Faire or Permissive Style - 'talks about emotions but doesn't give boundaries or set limits on behaviour'

Emotion Coaching style - 'Pause, Breathe, Connect, Engage with Empathy and Compassion, Problem Solve (with limit setting where necessary)'

'All emotions are OK but not all behaviours are OK'
Professor John Gottman

Emotion coaching validates emotions and feelings. Emotion coaching starts with the premise that talking about emotions is good and that asking children how they feel and listening to their responses enables the child's emotional development. Emotion coaching means noticing and commenting rather than trying to change the emotion or distract the child from what they are feeling. Boundaries are still important because although all emotions can be validated, not all behaviours need to be.

Emotion coaching is about building and enriching relationships

Teens and adolescents need us to maintain a 'consultant style' where we facilitate their transition into adulthood. Younger children need a 'managerial style' where we support them understand and describe their emotions.

Sarah has put together lots of free resources to help you learn about Mindful Emotion Coaching including e-learning modules, an e-book summary of the approach and a webpage full of useful video clips.

To access these resources go to www.mindfulemotioncoaching.co.uk

Personality, Neurodiversity and Stress

If your child is highly sensitive or has been diagnosed with a neuro-developmental difficulty such as high functioning autism you will find that you need to learn to notice when they are worrying about things or when they are sleeping poorly. Emotion coaching style relationships with adult caregivers are even more important for this group of children. You may find that noises hurt their ears more, that clothes seem really scratchy, or that bright sunshine makes their eyes ache. Sometimes doing deep mindful activities like sleeping under a weighted blanket, wearing a weighted jacket or rolling backwards and forwards on a ball can help them find their place of calm where they feel happy. Occupational therapists call this sensory integration.

Regular exercise helps our sensory systems stay balanced. Try and make sure as a parent or caregiver you do something EVERYDAY as part of your self-care. By doing this you are modelling the importance of self-care for your children.

As your child moves into adolesence you need to move from manager role to consultant role so that their brain can develop separately from yours. At this stage their friends become really important to them.

Having hobbies they can enjoy with their peers will support their emotional development.

Mindful Activities

Everyone uses their senses all of the time. Without our senses, we would not be able to interact with the world. Senses are things like sight, smell, taste, touch, balance, connection, inner body sensations eg. hunger. Our senses give us information and then our brain figures out what to do with it. Sometimes, this gets figured out just fine and we can make sense of the things that we see, we can move as we need to, we can enjoy tastes and smells, and so on. This is when we are balanced in the flow of our River of Wellbeing. However, sometimes, things don't work quite as smoothly. Sometimes, you may find yourself stuck on your Bank of Rigidity or on your Bank of Chaos. Mindful activities help us to spend more time in our River of Wellbeing.

A child's brain connects with the brains of their adult caregivers and develops in lots of different ways including something often called mirroring. Finding mindful activities we can do with our children helps us stay in our River of Wellbeing* and supports normal brain development.

*Dan Siegel and Tina Payne The Whole Brain Child Workbook page 10
© Mind Your Brain, Inc

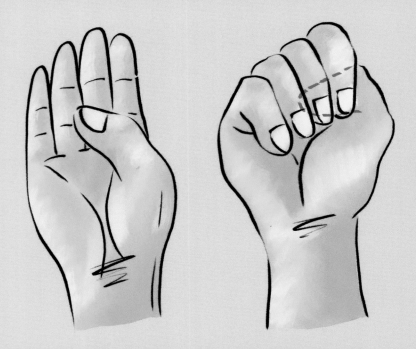

Integrating the Upstairs and Downstairs Brain

Professor Daniel J Siegel, The Whole Brain Child, pages 62-63. Mind Your Brain ©Inc 2015.

In this model the downstairs brain contains the emotion part of the brain -represented by the thumb- and acts like an accelerator. The thinking part of the brain (upstairs brain) acts as a brake on emotions and is represented by the finger tips. When the downstairs brain is 'reactive' the thumb wobbles, the fingers flap up from the closed fist position and eventually the fingers flip right up and we have 'Flipped our Lid'. When the thumb is calm and the fist is closed (representing motorways of connections between different areas of the brain) we are responsive. This is when we make our best decisions. When our lid is down and we are interacting with others who also have their lid down we make our best collective decisions and choices.

We can learn to calm the reactivity of our brain through emotion coaching techniques and mindful exercises. This is also referred to as Vagal Tone. The vagus nerve travels from another part of the downstairs brain (the brain stem) to key organs in the body, doing things like lowering heart rate and breathing rate. www.mindfulemotioncoaching.co.uk

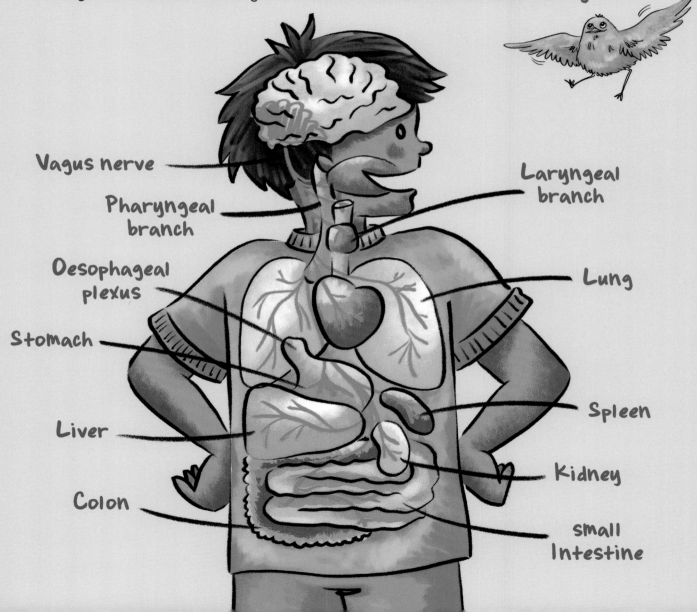

Vagus nerve

Pharyngeal branch

Laryngeal branch

Oesophageal plexus

Lung

Stomach

Liver

Spleen

Kidney

Colon

Small Intestine

If you are finding it hard to manage stress you may find you can get very emotional with your partner or with your children. In order to be able to manage an emotion coaching relationship style with others you may need some support managing your own emotions and behaviours.

Any of these things may make it more difficult for you to manage stress:

-mental health difficulties

-physical health difficulties

-experiencing trauma as an adult

-experiencing trauma as a child

-a significant bereavement

-being separated from family and friends

-loss of an income

Dr Sarah Temple and her learning community have produced a wide range of resources which you can access through this website;

www.mindfulemotioncoaching.co.uk

'This book has helped me understand what happens to children who can't regulate their emotions well and in turn has helped me to notice the signs when my daughter Ivy might be sad, worried or angry and to help her explore this and widen her vocabulary around her emotions. It's about helping children manage their emotions.

Many of us as children perhaps did not have the role models that helped us notice our feelings and we grew up deregulated and unaware of this neurological mis-wiring; and in turn as adults have had to turn to therapy to heal these wounds and have a mess of broken relationships around us not knowing why.

Is it not time to break this pattern?

Imagine having this tool as a child, being able to calm down your own nervous system and recognise the science within your own body. These tools are invaluable for all children and all family members- breaking down patterns and saving thousands in therapy and family break downs.' **Ivy's Mum, Somerset August 2020**

Glossary

Acute inflammatory phase
stimulation of the immune system protects the body from harmful things - often characterised by redness, swelling and pain

Adversity
a very difficult or unfavourable situation or experience

Brain architecture
billions of connections between individual brain cells across different areas of the brain

Chronic inflammatory phase
ongoing stimulation of the inflammatory phase of the immune system can eventually damage healthy cells

DNA
a molecule carrying genetic instructions

Emotion Coaching
validating, labelling and sitting with emotions when interacting with others

Epigenetics
an emerging area of scientific research showing how children's experiences affect the expression of their genes

Executive function and self-regulation skills
the mental processes that enable us to plan, focus attention, remember instructions, and juggle multiple tasks successfully. The brain needs this skill set to filter distractions, prioritise tasks, set and achieve goals, and control impulses